C000174047

# *Wh.* GREEN SPIRITUALITY?

Edited by
Marian Van Eyk McCain

With contributions by
Joan Angus, Niamh Brennan, Brendan Caulfield-James,
Michael Colebrook, Janice Dolley, Victoria Field,
Claudia Van Gerven, Malcolm Hollick, Mary Kelson,
Emily Kimball, Alison Leonard
and Susan Meeker-Lowry

Published by GreenSpirit
137 Ham Park Road, London E7 9LE
www.greenspirit.org.uk

Registered Charity No. 1045532

ISBN 978-0-9935983-5-7

Design and artwork by Stephen Wollaston (Santoshan)
Printed by CreateSpace and Amazon

Front cover photo © Beboy/Shutterstock.com

# CONTENTS

# PART ONE

# DEFINING GREEN
# SPIRITUALITY

# GREEN SPIRITUALITY

## Marian Van Eyk McCain

Some words stay still on the page when you write them.
Or if you think them they sit in your mind, like placid
babies, exactly where you put them. Words like 'giraffe' or
'lighthouse' that describe physical things are almost always
well-behaved, and even quite a few of the words we use to
describe vaguer and more conceptual ideas like 'cookery,'
'gardening' or 'psychiatry' are equally docile.

But there are some words that as soon as you begin to
write or think them immediately wriggle and squirm and
positively refuse to be pinned down. The word 'love' is a typical
example. Everybody knows what it means and yet nobody has
ever been able to give it one satisfactorily solid, comprehensive
definition. As soon as you try to, it slips away like a will o' the
wisp, impossible to grasp. Another such word is 'spirituality.'
What actually is it? We all think we know and yet we can't
quite explain. Not fully anyway.

For some people spirituality is synonymous with religion.
Yet there are millions of people who say they are 'spiritual but
not religious.' What does that actually *mean*? Once again, we
all know what it means, but how to explain it?

For me, the easiest and simplest way to define spirituality
is to describe it as a dimension of our lives. It is a dimension
that is every bit as real and vital and significant to us as

our physicality or our psychology. Yet it is a dimension that defies exact verbal or scientific analysis because, like a bird or a butterfly, you can feel the fluttering of its wings and enjoy its presence in your life but you cannot dissect it without killing it.

So let me start out with a warning. This is not a textbook. It is not an academic thesis or a philosophical treatise. My aim is not to dissect and analyse the topic the way a scientist or a lab technician would. It is not to present a set of facts to be learned. Think of it, rather, as a smorgasbord.

I realized years ago that when people were curious about my vegetarian diet the best way to answer them was not to respond with nutritional facts or persuasive arguments but to invite them to dinner. So my role here is more chef than teacher. I want to give you the flavour of green spirituality.

*The nun Wu Jincang asked the Sixth Patriach Huineng, "I have studied the Mahaparinirvana sutra for many years, yet there are many areas I do not quite understand. Please enlighten me."*
*The patriarch responded, "I am illiterate. Please read out the characters to me and perhaps I will be able to explain the meaning."*

*Said the nun, "You cannot even recognize the characters. How are you able then to understand the meaning?"*

*"Truth has nothing to do with words. Truth can be likened to the bright moon in the sky. Words, in this case, can be likened to a finger. The finger can point to the moon's location. However, the finger is not the moon. To look at the moon, it is necessary to gaze beyond the finger, right?"*

I have often heard poetry described like this, i.e. as a finger pointing to the moon. Following the direction of the finger means not dwelling too much on the precise meanings of the words themselves but reading between the lines, feeling the emotions that come through them. It means experiencing the words not with your intellect but with your heart and soul.

This book contains the pointing fingers of many different people. And my hope is that at least some of these people's descriptions of what green spirituality is and what it means to them personally will strike resonant chords within you.

So I am not going to spend any more time describing what spirituality is or isn't but I do need, before we start, to explain how I see the relationship of green spirituality to spirituality in general.

You will notice, if you look at any list of the world's various religions and spiritual paths, that 'green spirituality' per se is almost never included in the list. That is not because vast numbers of people don't follow some form of it. It is the opposite. It is because they *do*.

If you are classifying followers of all the world's religions and spiritual belief systems into a set of categories you cannot have a category for green spirituality, for the simple reason that there are millions of people in *all* the categories whose spirituality is green. In addition to the many millions of people who profess no adherence to any religion or who follow no specific spiritual path and yet whose beliefs and practices are actually very green, there are members of all traditions and persuasions whose deepest beliefs and daily actions fall under the heading of green spirituality. So there are green Hindus, green Buddhists, green

Christians, green Jews, green agnostics, green atheists…and so on. And they are all on a spectrum from very light green to very dark green, depending on how deeply they identify themselves as being an integral part of the planet which in turn is an integral part of an ever-evolving universe and also the degree to which they 'walk their talk.' For example, a true Christian will walk his or her talk by following the principles of peace, love, social justice and compassion towards others that were preached and modelled by Jesus Christ. Likewise, someone whose spirituality is dark green will love the Earth, feel at home in the universe, experience reverence for all Creation, advocate both social *and* *ecological* justice, have compassion for *all* living things, respect the wisdom and integrity of Nature (including its natural structures such as rocks and rivers) and believe in the intrinsic value of all life forms. Plus, such a person will almost certainly live a simple, sustainable, peaceful life with a very low eco-footprint.

Thus, as well as green spirituality not being a category, we cannot even call it a meta-category. Once again, we are talking about a dimension. And that is why you won't find it on the lists of belief systems.

On many of the lists you will find Paganism, because that is a category. In many lists—such as in the latest UK census—it is counted as a religion. However, 'Pagan' is another slippery word and one that even practising pagans often find it hard to define, since its origins are so ancient and so varied, including umpteen forms of animism (a belief in Nature spirits), polytheism (a belief in many gods), pantheism (a belief that the divine dwells within everything, including humans, i.e. immanent spirituality), panentheism (a belief that the divine is both within us and beyond us, i.e. transcendent spirituality) plus shamanism and various Nature-based belief systems of indigenous peoples, past and present.

One of the reasons that we cannot simply put all forms of green spirituality in the Paganism category is that nowadays it is understood by most people either as an umbrella term for such things as Druidism, Wicca and Celtic revivalist spiritual practices or as a way of denoting opposition to the Abrahamic religions such as Christianity, Islam and Judaism.

The spirituality of all Pagans is, by definition, green, since it is totally Earth-based. But not all Pagans walk the green talk and not everyone whose spirituality is based on a deep love of— and identification with—the Earth and its ecosystems wants to be classified as a Pagan, even if s/he has no other religious affiliations, since that generally implies a connection with one or another of the neo-paganist groups that have sprung up since the 19th Century. Overall, there are far more Buddhists, Christians and others with green spiritual beliefs and dark green lifestyles than there are self-professed Pagans. Plus there are several forms of Eastern spirituality, for example Shinto and Taoism, which are totally green yet have no connection whatsoever with the Paganism of the West.

So you can see now, I hope, why 'green spirituality,' although it is probably one of the most prevalent forms of spirituality that exists, is also one of the most invisible, since there is no easy way to include it in a census. A census is a two-dimensional thing but we live in many more dimensions than two. Leading thinkers of our times, such as Ken Wilber, have shown how a 'theory of everything' would need to include at least eight dimensions, for with any fewer than that we would only ever see a partial view of anything. But for our purposes here, all we need to remember is that:

—spirituality is a dimension of our existence
—we experience it subjectively, as individuals, especially at certain times and in certain settings
—we can also *think about it* subjectively, as individuals. And describe ourselves in terms of it
—we can share it experientially with others, as in rituals
—we can analyse and describe it objectively, as I am attempting to do here.

My intention, in editing this book, is thus not only to analyse and describe but also to:

—convey some of the flavour of green spirituality by having a few people recount their subjective, individual experiences in their own words
—stimulate you to examine your own beliefs and think objectively about how green or otherwise they are
—encourage you to share the green, spiritual dimension of your life with like-minded people, and
—inspire you, on behalf of our beautiful but beleaguered planet to turn your own beliefs and practices a darker shade of green.

So let's look first at beliefs.

## Origins

Green spirituality—a spirituality centred on this planet Earth, which is the only home we humans and our ancestors have ever known—is without a doubt the oldest form of spirituality in existence. And it has taken many, many forms. It probably began, as our species first evolved a capability for self-reflexive consciousness, with a wondering, a pondering, and the search for a story that would make sense of existence. Almost certainly, those first stories would have been based very much on what those early humans could see around them.

Besides the ground on which they stood, ancient peoples have also incorporated the sun, the moon and other celestial bodies into their spiritual stories and creation myths, along with many of Earth's wild creatures, its mountains, lakes, rivers and forests, finding sacred meaning in many aspects of Nature. 'Who or what are we?' 'Where did we come from?' and 'Why are we here?' are ancient, universal questions and there are as many answers as there are—and have been—human cultures.

Although the various religious traditions all have their own versions of the creation story, we in the Western world had never had one central story that almost all of us could fully subscribe to until, in our modern times, science began to reveal our planet's true history and its gradual transformation from a ball of flame into a blue, white and gold jewel in the solar system, redolent with life. Geologian Thomas Berry and cosmologist Brian Swimme have retold this story beautifully in their book *The Universe Story*, bringing us all the way from what they term "The primordial flaring forth" up to the new, green phase of history we are now entering, which they call the Ecozoic Era.

We are living right on the cusp of this momentous change. There has never been a more exciting and creative time to be alive.

Of course the more we learn, the more we realize we don't know. There are many mysteries still to solve about the true nature of the universe, mysteries we may never get to the bottom of. At least, however, we now have some satisfying answers to the first two questions—what we are and where we came from—and we are starting to suggest some tentative answers to the third: why are we here? If indeed humans do have a task, a role, a part to play in the great unfolding of evolution, what is it to be?

Many of us today look back at earlier answers to this question and feel a huge regret that, in the Western world at least, both science and religion conspired to give us a false sense of our own importance. This widespread assumption that *Homo sapiens* is in some way 'superior' to all other life forms, has led to a selfish disregard for the rest of creation. It has caused us to plunder our planet's finite resources and to create such disequilibrium that we have even caused changes in our climate. Our modern values have become anthropocentric ('man'-based) instead of ecocentric.

It may not feel like it sometimes, but there are many signs that the tide is beginning to turn. Finally—and maybe only in the nick of time—we are starting to wake up. The dramatic loss of species like bees, for example, is forcing us to realize that if we are talking 'importance' there are many creatures who play a much more vital and important part in our ecosystems than we do. Earthworms are another example. And most forms of bacteria. We could never do what they do and they are far more 'important' to the planet's healthy functioning than we are. We depend on them, whereas they scarcely depend on us at all. We may, in fact, be the only form of life that is totally expendable since none of the other life forms actually *need* us, and even the ones well-adapted to our presence such as rats, cockroaches, body lice and gut bacteria would soon find new places to live and work.

What a humbling thought! We probably need a dose of humility, as a counter to the hubris we have shown up to now. But after all, we are a young species and youngsters are naturally narcissistic. The task of growing out of our narcissistic phase is a developmental one. So let's not waste time blaming our ancestors or ourselves and instead let's move on, into the Ecozoic Era.

But how? Again we ask "Why are we here? Do humans even *have* a role in the great scheme of things and in the process of evolution?" Maybe we do. And in the next part Niamh Brennan will give you some of her thoughts on what that role might be.

\*   \*   \*

# PART TWO

# HUMANS

# BEING HUMAN

## Niamh Brennan

What is this life for? Seven million years in existence and still the human being as individual and the human species as collective cannot answer this question. There are some who believe that they know and who prioritise belief over fact. There are some who 'know' and prioritise fact over belief but ultimately with all the power of our searching and yearning, curious souls, 'life' in its essence and in its purpose and even though we are in its midst and living it, remains elusive to us. It is beyond our grasp of comprehension. It is mystery. What if we were to accept the mystery of life? To think that although we know much we do not nor perhaps cannot know all. What if that were the premise from which we started to think about life—as ultimately shrouded in mystery, its deeper meaning hidden to us but with the seed of its desire planted so firmly in us that we are constantly driven to seek? And although life and its meaning might remain a mystery to us there are some things that we can learn about and know—this beautiful planet, our Earth.

Miriam Therese MacGillis writes how it took over four billion years of

*increasing complexity and diversification for the Earth to unfold within itself a brain so highly evolved, a nervous system so highly organised, a skeletal structure so highly developed, that the Earth became capable not only of living and breathing, moving, feeding, reproducing itself, of seeing and hearing, but now it had evolved an organism so complex that the Earth became capable of thinking about itself. And that's the human.*

What can the Earth teach us? What does a time developmental story, beginning 13.7 billion years ago, a story that is unfolding and emerging, increasing in complexity of form and complexity of consciousness, teach us about what it means to be human and what the human life is for? What can it tell us about the role of the human being, how we should be, how we should act and what is our place?

**Witness**

The last 65 million years of Earth's history have been one of its most productive, a time of mesmerising creativity where the Earth flowered in bright and blazing colours, where the grasses spread and the forests rose stoic and serene. The Earth gave birth to the whale, the dolphin, the monkey and the elephant and the butterfly. She gave birth to the rosebush and the lilac tree and the jasmine vine perfuming the planet with their intoxicating scents until eventually with an imagination and a spirit shaped by the beauty of her creatures, the bounty of her fruits, and the majesty of her shape and colour, she gave birth to our species. And through us her ability to admire herself. The Human Being in some curious manner is the Earth living herself, experiencing herself and watching and observing her own many manifestations. We bear witness to all that the

Earth is, that the divine is, marvel and tremble at her powers, her generosity, her abundance, her terrors; she has allowed us to participate in her, taste her, experience her, allowed us in some way to know her. And how do we best do this? Through silent observation, through reverence and consideration of all, through humility at taking part in this great gift of life.

Have you ever listened to a bird's song and wondered what he is declaring, who he is singing to? Have you ever watched a snail come out after the rain, her house on her back and wondered why the rain stirs her so, or watched the weeping willow as the wind passes through her and wondered what she felt? Every creature has a story to tell, a journey they have made, a wisdom to share; every creature is, in the words of Meister Eckhart, "a book about God." And as we watch and bear witness to these creatures, perhaps we can learn once again how to be part of Nature, how to relate to the other species we share the planet with. Perhaps we can learn to let go of the existential angst that has come to be associated with being human: the rage and frustration that comes with our human limitations, our futile and destructive competitiveness. Perhaps we can learn gratitude for the mysterious gift that life is, despite its sufferings and disappointments and brevity. Perhaps we can learn that the divine is fully present in us, present and living on this Earth and beating in our own fragile heart, dependent on our eyes to see her, our ears to hear her and our lives to proclaim and rejoice her. Perhaps then our heart will open up to the mystery and we shall realise that our role is to celebrate what is here, was here before us and will be after us and to praise it and wonder about it and be in awe and gratitude of it.

## The Collective Mind

And as we witness we are learning. We are learning about our Earth from the symbols and information and feelings and thoughts and creation that she is unfolding to us, that she is also unfolding within us. Slowly we have learned of her many transformations, her differentiation of form and the elegance of her complex cells. We have documented and recorded what we are learning and passed it on so that those who come after us may also add to it. We are helping to build a picture of what this Earth and this Universe is, a picture that has been changed and modified as we have learnt more, a picture that even as we assemble it, contains us.

We are yet to learn the full potential of technology or machines, the full potential of what we are creating. And yet, as human beings, create we must and so with or against our will, we are creating a mind fashioned by history and culture, by the sweeping winds and spirit of change, a mind that is stored in books and technology and instruments, and in the human being. And perhaps this is what the human species is here to do, to complete and reflect back what the Universe—and our Earth as part of it—itself is creating. Ever more complex, ever more diverse, ever more spiritual, going somewhere, building something. And maybe that is us, in the same way that it is every creature, but with the particular form of consciousness given us, perhaps it is ours to help unveil the mystery, to make the divine more transparent through description, explanation and representation of her creation.

## Personalisation

I know that it is not for one person to write about what is the place of the human being. It is not for one person to stand outside her species, who presently number 7 billion, and to say what this species is on Earth for and what are its contribution to life, to this planet and to the Universe. Each person can only offer insight and wisdom from their own experience, can only give an opinion, even though learned and studied and researched, an opinion nonetheless, which no matter how we try, always remains personal. Mine is that as we cannot escape our own personhood, as we can never exist separate from it, that perhaps this is the key—to become as personal and as integrated as we can in order that we may reflect the Earth, express it and experience it, admire it in our own unique way. In order that we may personalise it.

The French priest and palaeontologist, Pierre Teilhard de Chardin wrote about "the personalising universe." He wrote that it is the task of each of us, "to establish in ourselves an absolutely original centre where the universe is reflected in a unique and inimitable way: precisely our self, our personality." On a planet that thrives on diversity and differentiation, we must not be afraid of what makes us different but seek to deepen it, understand it and love it. And eventually when we are accepting of the realisation that we do not think the same, nor love the same, nor understand the same, then we must express that which is only of us, gift it back to the Earth from whence it came and add to the kaleidoscope and tapestry that life is. Add the deepest awareness and expression of our own self—a life lived from its depths.

Rilke in *Letters to a Young Poet* also writes,

*Think, dear Sir, of the world which you carry within yourself, and call this thinking what you like; let it be memory of your own childhood or longing for your own future—only pay attention to what arises within you, and set it above everything you notice about you. Your inmost happening is worth your whole love.*

Our development and authenticity as a person must come from the exploration of our own interior depths, from the deep solitude and silence wherein we can hear God speak and learn how we must speak, where the noises and voices that are constant in our mind are silenced until we arrive in the place beyond thought, beyond knowledge, beyond the separate self. In this place lies whatever it was that breathed the fireball into existence; that transformed hydrogen and helium into stars, and star dust into planets and peoples. The same essence that shines the moon and grows the sunflower, that forgives a failing and kisses a child. The same essence that is seeking to create again; the essence that is seeking to be known. It is unique to each one of us and in its expression creates a community richer for its diversity and tolerance.

Too often, we speak of professionalism and efficiency. We pay homage to these concepts and seek to imbibe and reproduce them, make them our aim. But what is professionalism but the increased mechanisation of someone, where we sacrifice feelings of solidarity and compassion in order to become the most efficient cog in the corporate machine. Our human role is not to be professional but to be as human as we can, as fully human as we possibly can. Feeling others, loving others, caring for others, serving others, being foolish and vulnerable and making as many mistakes in our short lives as we possibly can. Is there anything more human than to make a mistake? Doesn't the universe itself as it unfolds its mighty self, grope and chance and make mistakes? Personalisation is to feel and to know my own centre, the centre that beats in me but also beats in every one else and to live and to love and to breathe out of this centre knowing that there is no model for anybody's life, no instruction manual, no map or blueprint to follow, only the seed that lies in the depths of us waiting to be discovered, waiting to bloom in us.

Our destiny as a species is dependent on each person coming to know their own centre in order that they might contribute to the whole. And so we embrace the pain and the suffering for the lessons these must teach us, we embrace the joys and the hopes and the mystery that is our existence. We take them all gratefully and celebrate them and live them through as fully and as compassionately and as thoughtfully as we can. With every life adding a new dimension to joy and a new dimension to pain, deepening the feeling of the Earth, adding to its depth, increasing its creativity, increasing its love, giving flesh to its spirit and completing the whole.

## Conclusion
The human being—a unique manifestation of the Earth that flounders in our role. We need to remember who we are, to think beyond competition, to think beyond consumption, to

become who we were born to be, holding the consciousness that reflects the Earth, personalising it, praising it. We need to remember our every action has a consequence, sometimes immediately noticeable, sometimes taking a lifetime to manifest. It is all tied together, one seamless event—how could it not be? This is not fate or fatalism but rather a thread that runs through life, a thread that *is* life, and which we pull and tug, causing effect and consequence. This world that took so long to bring us forth, to create us, is now the very host that we are destroying. The Native Americans speak about thinking for seven generations. Can we do that? Can we think beyond the lives of our own children or our children's children? What planet are we bequeathing to them? In the midst of this economic recession and the difficulty of these times lies the opportunity to think about where we have come from, how we have come to be, to re-claim our identity and refashion our destiny and in doing so birth a species that is worthy of this universe and worthy of this planet, home.

\*     \*     \*

# PART THREE

# GREENSPIRIT

# A BRIEF OVERVIEW

Marian Van Eyk McCain

---

There are very few organizations that I know of which define themselves as being about green spirituality of all kinds rather than being part of one religion or spiritual tradition. But there is at least one such organization and Niamh and I are part of it. So are some of the other contributors to this book, though not all. It is called GreenSpirit and it is based in the UK although in recent years—particularly since the publication of our book *GreenSpirit: Path to a New Consciousness*—it is attracting increasing numbers of people from around the world. GreenSpirit started out, back in the 1980s, as a vehicle for the pioneering work of radical American theologian Matthew Fox and his creation-centred spirituality (i.e. spirituality that was centred in the wonder and joy of being alive on this beautiful planet, in the way that Niamh just described, rather than focused on some imagined Heaven beyond death) but it soon expanded to include many other ideas and to promulgate the writings of many other influential writers, particularly Thomas Berry. Here is Brendan Caulfield James to tell you more about GreenSpirit, what it is and what it stands for.

\*    \*    \*

31

# WHAT ON EARTH IS GREENSPIRIT?

Brendan Caulfield-James

I am often asked, "What is GreenSpirit?" and find it difficult to answer. The first challenge I face is the word 'green' itself, which conjures up a cauldron of conflicting images.

The Green Man of forests, pubs and traffic lights. The greenhorn, green-behind-the-ears novice. The agonised green-with-envy person at another's perceived better fortune. The overindulgent reveller turning 'green around the gills' after a night out on the town. Those ubiquitous greenies lobbying on behalf of the environment. The verdant lushness of Spring. The safety of Basra's Green Zone. The green belt as opposed to the brown one. The 17th of March, when faces, drinks and even waterways turn green in honour of St. Patrick, apostle of the Emerald Isle. Putting greens on golf courses, except in the Australian outback where they are black. Green mould that tells us, if our noses don't, that the cheese is getting past its use-by date. The Green Berets and Green Jackets among the ranks of our armed forces. The colour itself and its subtle variations. A green planet before flowers introduced other colours. I could go on…

There was a time when we specified what we meant. Our spirituality was described as 'creation centred.' Though a bit of a tongue-twister, the phrase conveyed what it said. Until, that is, 'Creationism' (a literal interpretation of the Biblical accounts of creation) reared its ugly head and spread its toxic tentacles. The waters became muddied. Even those from whom we would have expected greater discernment began lumping us both in the same basket. So we retreated and opted for 'GreenSpirit' instead, which, it must be said, has a more appealing ring to it, even if it is hard to describe.

This brings me to the second term, the word 'Spirit.' For many, this suggests an otherworldly dimension that is both distinct from and opposed to the material world which we inhabit. I was brought up in a religious tradition that sought fulfilment in a life hereafter, not this one. Yet paradoxically, being rooted in creation, our spirituality is integrally materialistic. The Ash Wednesday ritual of daubing ash on foreheads, while chanting "Remember you are earth and unto earth you will return," reminds us of our origin and destiny in created reality. There is no duality between matter and spirit, except in some minds. All matter is inspirited. Where else, except from creation, do we find symbols and derive rituals that inspire and nurture our spirits? Beltane, the Pagan festival of Spring, exuberantly celebrates this union of spirit and matter. When I ask other 'greenspirits' for their views on green spirituality, their answers vary widely. But one thread that links them all is our embeddedness in the natural world.

"In the natural world," writes Thomas Berry, "we discover the mysterious power whence all things come into being." He goes on to suggest that we leave our bibles on their shelves for twenty years and learn instead to read the scriptures of Nature.

For the natural world is the sacred community into which we are born, by which we are nourished and from which we find wisdom.

I grew up in a city, loved it and could not imagine anywhere better. It was my choice of career on leaving school that changed all that. Suddenly I found myself isolated for long periods of time in the middle of the vast Bog of Allen in the Irish midlands. The forests and lakes, rivers and skies, fauna and flora, unique to this geographical region, began slowly to infiltrate my awareness. Almost unconsciously, I found myself going for walks in the countryside, discovering an enchanting and exhilarating environment. I realised then I had fallen in love with a magical universe that was gifted to me at birth. I experience each day now as a new awakening. I go to sleep at night anticipating a dawn of more fascinating and thrilling discoveries. I feel truly blessed.

I even get excited by things like bluebells which once I scarcely noticed. Recently, tipped off by a friend, I discovered The Hollies, a nearby wood, aglow with the subdued colours and perfumed by the subtle scent of bluebell clusters.

It is awesome to reflect that the arrival of flowers like these started the revolution of the Cenozoic Age, which witnessed the most prolific flourishing of life forms on this planet. And sad to realise that we are living in its terminal phase, due largely to human intervention.

For me, GreenSpirit is about love and gratitude. Seeing the world as blessing, learning to love it and seeking to share it with others. The longer I live, the more I realise how privileged I am to be here. Every moment is a '*Carpe diem!*' moment to be seized. Berry was asked in an interview if he practised meditation. With a chuckle he replied that he probably did not do so formally. Then added that he had a dream life and a waking life that went on simultaneously. I find this encouraging. I do have my sacred space—a rustic bench by a quiet pond in the countryside. I go there in my imagination whenever I need to. There I can relax, tune in to an inner wisdom and connect to the real world. The rest of the time I fluctuate between different states of consciousness as required to survive!

But there is more to GreenSpirit. I find Matthew Fox's Four Paths of Creation Spirituality a helpful compass. The first path, *Via Positiva*, can be described as the state of being in love with life. This is fundamental to my efforts to address the current environmental crisis. Love is, after all, the prime motivator. Because I feel passionate about our planet, I want to thrive with it, not perish. The second path, *Via Negativa*, points to how life's travails are part of a progressive journey. A few years ago, I went through a bad patch and was hospitalised for four months. This turned out to be one of the greatest favours of my life. I emerged from the experience with batteries recharged and a fresh outlook. As part of Nature, we are not exempt from the cycle of dying and rising we observe around us in the changing seasons. The third path, *Via Creativa*, reveals our creative potential, the greatest expression of our divine nature and the most neglected. We ignore it at our peril. José Hobday, Native American and Franciscan nun, urges us to get green "by reaching in to the veins of all creation, to the arteries that pulse with a heart that is bigger than ours." Finally, the fourth path, *Via Transformativa*, propels us into those transformative experiences that result from engaging with the world, rather than burying our heads in the sand. This is particularly poignant for me at the moment, as I attempt to connect with the land through growing food.

Perhaps, after all, the 'green' in GreenSpirit is the most apt expression of a spirituality for our time. Hildegard of Bingen urges us to get green in spirit. This recalls a period when early life on Planet Earth was running out of food. Out of this apparent crisis, creative cells invented the chlorophyll molecule which enabled them to capture light from the Sun and transform it into energy. Photosynthesis came to the rescue. A new partnership with the Sun provided the food and energy for life to prosper.

Is there a message of hope in this for a planet under assault and a people facing extinction? Early tribal societies faced environmental crises before by strengthening their inner world, not seeking to alter the outer. In one Native American creation story, Woman wakes up first to find Man asleep beside her and wonders how to wake him, while the Creator and Coyote watch from behind a tree. To their surprise, she decides to tickle him! As José Hobday once said: "Let's find out what can make creation laugh instead of crying this acid rain all the time and shedding tears of destruction into the soil!"

\*   \*   \*

# PART FOUR

# EPIPHANIES

# FALLING IN LOVE
# WITH GAIA

Susan Meeker-Lowry

M y personal introduction to the Gaia Hypothesis—the idea first put forward by scientists James Lovelock and Lyn Margulis and supported by good evidence, that the Earth itself might actually be a living being—was in November 1985. It was my second visit to the Chinook Learning Center, an intentional community and educational center on Whidbey Island in Washington State, USA, founded by former residents of the Findhorn community in Scotland. I was participating in Chinook's conference, 'For the Life of the Earth,' to learn about new projects and to share ideas. I arrived a bit late for the first gathering on Friday evening and Thomas Berry, author, priest, and cultural historian, had just started speaking. His eyes twinkled with good humor and he was full of energy and passion as he spoke of the importance of integrating ecology and spirit into politics, economics... and everything else. His wasn't simply an intellectual understanding of the topic. I could tell he felt the magic of the Earth in every cell of his body. It wasn't just what he said, it was how he said it. I was entranced.

One of the topics he discussed was the Gaia Hypothesis. My heart immediately embraced the idea. As Thomas spoke, the pieces fell into place. He put words on what I'd known intuitively all my life. Tears came to my eyes, hope grew in my heart, and my mind reeled with the implications. I thought about the role love plays in the healing process, how it works miracles, speeding recovery from illness and nourishing the spirits of people and animals alike. 'Healing the Earth' was a common phrase, but it seemed so arrogant. How could we possibly heal the Earth? But, if the Earth is alive then love is an important part of the healing process. And if love is part of the healing process then we can make a difference. What we do and how we do it matters. We may be David acting against a powerful Goliath, but we have Gaia, a living being, on our side! Nothing has been the same for me since.

There are many books available designed to help us reconnect with Nature and our human nature as well. Some are intellectual and theoretical, others are experiential, and still others read more like stories. While I know it takes more than a book to change someone, I also know that a good book read at the right time can touch us and make a difference. Sometimes the right words—like Thomas Berry describing the Gaia Hypothesis all those years ago—help us articulate a feeling or confirm an intuition.

But our minds and intellects can take us only so far. To understand Gaia, to let her into our lives, we must fall in love with the Earth. It's that simple. We must love the Earth with the same passion and concern and fierceness that we love our children, our parents, our lovers, our mates. As anyone who has ever fallen in love knows, logic and reason have little to do with it. Sometimes we resist, but it happens anyway. Sometimes the object of our love seems totally wrong to others, but it doesn't matter. We love regardless. And the love we feel for our children—it is totally unconditional. This is the way we must love the Earth because this is the kind of love that changes everything. When we love someone we want the best for them. We make mistakes, yes, but once we realize what we've done we try to do better next time.

When we love someone, we don't deliberately set out to destroy or undermine them or jeopardize their chances at life. When they are hurt we yearn to hold and comfort them, and we know that our love makes a difference. Sometimes love is all there is, and it's enough.

The best way to fall in love with the Earth is to experience her. On a basic level, of course, every breath we take connects us to the Earth. So does the food we eat, the water we drink and bathe in (and flush down the toilet). The leather in our shoes, the cotton or wool or silk of our clothes, the paper we take notes on, etc. The point is to increase our awareness, to remind ourselves often of how we depend on the Earth, how we couldn't survive without her. Remember—we live IN Gaia. We eat, sleep, read, take the bus, drive our cars, and dispose of our trash IN Gaia.

The implications of Gaia Theory are immense and touch every aspect of human behaviour, from science to politics to commerce to social services. Nothing is exempt. We're coming full circle. In the beginning, gods and goddesses reigned and myth and stories explained the meaning of life and guided human behaviour. As our knowledge of Nature and the human body expanded, life was reduced to its material parts and the magic, the indefinable essence of being alive, was discounted and even feared. Science became the new god and the goddess was banished. Gaia helps us integrate the stories of the ancients with the stories of modern science into a cohesive whole and restores wonder and magic and mystery to our lives. The path to Gaia Theory may have been scientific inquiry, but the path to Gaia is through the heart.

*       *       *

**Publisher's Note**

This is an extract from a longer article entitled *Gaia in Our Hearts*, first published in Spirit of Change magazine in Jan/Feb 2002. It is reprinted here with the author's permission.

# BUILDING BRIDGES: AN IMPERATIVE OF EVOLVING CONSCIOUSNESS

Janice Dolley

---

This is the time of our calling as a species to remember the essential oneness that underpins all life and deepen the connections that will help us transcend and include apparent difference.

My own awakening to the reality of the One Life happened dramatically and suddenly in the early 1970s when, sitting in a secluded part of the garden to meditate, away from children playing, it was as though a curtain went back on reality and I saw the shimmer of energy dancing—everywhere. It was expressing here as a bush, there as a bud, there a wasp and here as me. I also 'knew' beyond any rational thought that this energy was totally loving and the beneficent source of all. That experience proved to be a turning point in my life. 40 years later I am still doing my best to bring this through as a reality in my own life and in the world.

Then, shortly after that garden experience I realized that there are seven major paths, or traditions, or ways of seeing the world and we have to build the bridges between these paths. We cannot return into the Oneness without being one in both consciousness and action.

So, like many others awakening to the 'new' inter-connected consciousness I sought out people who were feeling a similar impulse within. Together we created an association of those also seeing the need for deeper connections with each other, with the 'God' within and with all created life. We quickly realised that, important as ideas can be, they needed to be grounded in practical action so we clubbed together and set about farming organically, creating community and educating ourselves and others on the implication of living in a holistic way. It was a brave experiment as, I guess, have been the early steps in biological evolution. The impulse to evolve flows through us and we respond as best we can. The farm and its associated educational centre lasted about eight years. Its ending was brought about through financial and interpersonal stresses and also through the lack of experience and professionalism in animal management. By the time it ended, a start was being made by others on what was to become Friends of the Earth, and the pioneering work of the Findhorn Foundation. So, whilst the farm focus was no longer there we maintained the association for purposes of linking up and learning and kept a small patch of the farm woodland with a meditation hut and a small chalet for day visits and retreat.

*The old order changeth, yielding place to new,*
*And God fulfils himself in many ways*
*Lest one good custom should corrupt the world*
—Tennyson

Deep within the vision that sustains us is the knowing that our commission as humans at this stage in our evolutionary journey is not just to build bridges between people, faiths and ideas; not just to connect deeply with all manifestations of the creative impulse in the mineral, vegetable and animal kingdoms, but also to work towards "thy kingdom come on earth as in heaven." This involves also connecting with other dimensions of being and bringing through the lived oneness of 'heaven' onto this earth plane of our wondrously beautiful planet. As Matthew Fox once said, "We come together as participants in an ongoing and unfolding universe."

As part of the natural world that has been evolving over four and a half billion years, we contribute our new understanding of the oneness of all life and we embrace the whole.

We are now remembering the story of the Universe: from that first primordial flaring forth until this present moment, every star that has been born and died, every whirling galaxy and every atom, every life form that has come and gone, every earthworm, every cabbage, all great forests that have covered the planet, each unique sunrise and sunset, dance and rhythm, music, art and poetry, all human emotions, all spirituality and spiritualities, the questioning human mind, the rise of consciousness. All, without exception, are an inseparable part of the ongoing story.

We are now not merely surveying the universe from a conceptual point 'outside' of it. Slowly now we are realizing that we *are* the Universe itself reflecting on itself. We know deep within us that, as Alexander Pope tells us, we are "…part of one stupendous whole, whose body Nature is, and God the soul."

We know now that our unrelated separateness is an illusion and as we begin to see differently we face the great reality of our inter-connectedness and understand what we were told that "You and I are One even as the Father and I are One".
In the words of Christopher Fry, "It takes a thousand, thousand years to wake" but, alleluia—we are now awakening. One by one, one by one, we come to remember, we connect, converge and join in co-creating the ongoing dance of life.

*   *   *

# I HAVE BEEN A FOUR-LEGGED ANIMAL

## Alison Leonard

A darkened room. A group of fifteen people who don't know each other. Quiet. The leader speaks for about five minutes, telling us about the tiny figurines found on archaeological sites, the postures they show, the idea that these figurines might be aids to trance, the research by someone eminent showing that the method can be used in modern times. She seems sensible, and has conveyed a certain sense of trust.

I'm not sure why I'm here. I signed on because the title of the workshop, 'Trance Postures' sounded interestingly wacky and I thought I could spare a couple of hours in the middle of the conference. I put my arms in the required position (the postures are simple, not uncomfortable) and close my eyes.

The leader starts to drum. A steady beat. It will change our brain-waves. She will drum for 15 minutes. She will be interested in what we see.

The drum-beat enters my senses. Under my eyelids, I see bright lights in different colours. I'm aware that instead of letting my eyes rest and looking inward, I'm looking into my eyelids as though into a forward landscape. The light steadies to a rusty orange and starts to move across my vision from right to left; then it speeds up and begins to take the form of moving animals. A herd of deer, maybe, or wildebeest? More likely the latter—they're big.

I think, 'Yes, these are wildebeest,' and straightaway the words 'You've been watching too much David Attenborough!' run across my mind. I notice it and let it pass.

Yes, wildebeest—and there are thousands of them. A massive herd, in migration. I'm absorbed into the hammering, thundering movement of their hooves, the individual bodies moving as one, the dust they raise, the heat and sweat of this press and charge, the urgency of the process, its inevitability, like childbirth. I am part of the process. At the same time, I'm aware of my presence in this darkened room in a tall thin building off the main street of an English market town, of my bodily position, of the other people in the room, of the workshop that I'm a part of.

Now I become aware of my skeleton inside me. My spine, my thigh-bones, my pelvic circle, my skull. My jaw-bones! I feel the bone of my lower jaw being stretched forwards. My bone is changing from human to wildebeest. From my bones outwards, I'm becoming one of these wild animals as they run.

I'm one of the young ones, and not strong. We're being chased by a predator—I can't see what kind of predator it is, I'm racing too fast and with too harsh a sense of panic. I'm young, I'm fragile, I'm on the outside of the herd, I've lost my mother and I'm desperate with fear. I run, run, run....

And, in a shock instant, the back of my neck is seized in huge incisor teeth, in a massive jaw. I am caught. My entire head is jerked upward, my jaw jerked forward. I think, though I'm not sure (and I'm not asking any questions until afterwards), that the position of my human body doesn't change. I'm sitting as still as before, as still as the other people in this darkened room.

What happens next?

There's a gap in the film here. Yet it isn't a film. It's experience. The form, with its vivid sections separated by hiatuses, is like a dream. Yet it has the hardness, the definition, the coherence of experience. This is trance, trance experience.

I don't experience being killed and torn apart and eaten. Is it a defence of my brain, or the young wildebeest's brain, to be saved from remembering this agony?

The next scene is quiet and still. The herd, instead of charging in dust and sweat and panic, have arranged themselves in a huge silent circle. I am the young wildebeest still, but I'm no longer flesh, just bone and spirit. I am in two places at the same time: in the bones that are heaped in the centre of the circle of beasts, and, as spirit, hovering above the circle, gazing down at my grieving family and friends. I love them, and they love me. I know that they are expressing sorrow at their loss of me, and their gratitude for my sacrifice. If it had not been me who was offered to the predator, it would have been one of them. They will miss me.

The drum beat slows, and grows louder. It's time to come out of the trance, ease ourselves out of the postures, and rejoin everyday life. First we'll share our experiences in pairs, then we can speak to the leader, in the group or privately, about what we've seen.

I tell my partner what happened to me. It seems amazing to

hear it coming out of my mouth as a story. Yet it seems oddly ordinary too. It happened. It's over. My partner listens, and says she doesn't know what to say. I sympathise with her. I ask her what she saw during her 15 minutes, and she says, 'Nothing much, a few colours.' Later, aside from the group, I tell the leader about being a wildebeest caught by a predator and being grieved for by my herd. She's fascinated, and asks if she can quote me. I never see her again, and it's a couple of years before I even read the book on which the practice is based.

But I am changed. I know that I was once a different kind of animal, wild, a member of a herd. Somewhere inside me, the spirit and even the bone-memory of that wildebeest still lives. I have a different view of the human place in the scheme of things, and, very slowly, that different view begins to change my life.

*    *    *

**Note**

The research on which this workshop was based is *Where the Spirits Ride the Wind*, by Felicitas Goodman, published 1990 by Indiana University Press, ISBN 0-253-20566-2

# MEETING THE GOLDEN ONE

Emily Kimball

I dig my hiking poles into the dirt and push myself forward, stopping to catch my breath as I climb slowly skyward. Gazing up at the mountains I wonder if I can make it all the way. The higher I climb the shorter my breath; I pause often to rest and gobble down energy bars. Would I be able to finish this 11 ½ mile vertical hike in Sequoia National Park with my friends from the Old Dominion Appalachian Trail Club?

Our eight member group started out early in the morning, fully aware of the 2000 foot elevation change ahead of us. The mules hauling our equipment to the mountain campsite are following a different route. We carry only day packs with rain gear, extra clothes, snacks and water.

As we move up the trail the sun is shining and the mountains surrounding us shoot up into the sky—huge impenetrable bastions of solid gray rock, harboring rushing waterfalls, and spotted with the white glow of glacial ice. We are climbing higher and higher, the mountains close in and I feel nose to nose with them. Relief flows through me as the trail turns and a flat wooded area stretches invitingly ahead.

As I enter the forest I realize that I am hiking in the middle of our group. My friend Jim and co-leader Ben are behind—the others are way ahead. I am feeling a little nervous that perhaps I have lost my way. I hear a sudden rustling in the underbrush about 50 feet ahead to the right of the trail. What is that? My eyes strain to see the cause of this sudden movement. I search the shrubbery and see an animal moving in the bushes…it is yellowish. My God could it be a mountain lion? I stand riveted to the trail, legs trembling, heart pounding, breaths coming in short gasps. I have been warned about mountain lions. "Don't run. They will think you are prey and chase you. Don't hike alone they are more apt to maybe eat you!" What a way to go—devoured by a mountain lion!

Suddenly the creature moves into fuller view and I realize it isn't a mountain lion. It is too big. A mountain lion is the size of a large cat. This animal is much bigger. It certainly is yellow though—a beautiful golden yellow. What large animal would be sporting such a bright color? Couldn't be a bear. Bears aren't yellow. Sequoia has black bears. I examine the golden colored creature more carefully. He is nose down on all fours slowly pawing the underbrush searching for food. The black skin of his ears and nose stands out from his bright golden fur. I stop dead in my tracks and gasp. Indeed, it is a bear, a huge one, and yes, it *is* golden.

At first I am frightened at being alone with a bear in the wilderness. Knowing that unless cubs are nearby, or you have food, bears have no interest in people helps to keep me calm. If I make noise I know he will run away. The excitement and thrill of this unique opportunity to observe a bear in the wild grabs me. I cautiously back up, and then tiptoe forward to observe him. I don't want to scare him off before I get a good look. I have never seen a yellow bear before! He is definitely an adult, very large and the color of goldenrod. He is rambling along in the under-brush head down, his limbs moving laboriously as he inches along. If he knows a human being is invading his territory he never lets on. I stand there watching him for a full five minutes, my eyes following his every movement. I marvel at the size and majesty of this regal creature. I become totally transfixed and at one with the bear, forgetting any fear as I enter into this exquisite meet-up in Nature.

Presently Jim and Ben come along. Putting my finger to my lips I whisper, "There's a gorgeous yellow bear ahead." Just then he crosses the trail in front of us and lumbers off into the woods. I shall never forget the beauty of his golden fur sliding like a waterfall over his giant skeleton, and the rhythm of his gait as he trotted off into the wild. I learned later from the Ranger that I had seen a black bear. Black bears, he explained, just like people, have children with yellow hair, red hair, brown hair…

I have seen bears before on my many trips into the wilderness. But this meet-up, by myself, high in the mountains of Sequoia National Park, with a *golden* bear topped all of my other bear experiences.

I am a Quaker and really feel at home with the Quaker principles of simplicity, peace, care of the environment, but I get my real nurturing from being out in Nature. Hiking takes me into myself and away from my daily concerns. It is the way I rejuvenate my soul from the pressures of life. I think I get more from the silence of the trail than I get from the silence of Quaker meeting to be honest. Yes, Nature is my true religion.

\*     \*     \*

# PART FIVE

# IMMANENCE
# TRANSCENDENCE
# INSCENDENCE

# THE FLOWERING OF SPIRITUALITY

## Malcolm Hollick

It's Easter Sunday as I start to write. Here in the north of Scotland, Spring's resurrection is in full flow. I kneel, worshipping, as gently and with thanks I ease winter weeds from the ground and speed their transformation back to soil. With blessings, I welcome the less vigorous harbingers of summer's glory. With joy I greet crocus and tulip, primula and pansy, aubrietia, polyanthus, broom and berberis.

In the woods, buds swell, split, unfold; new growth thrusts through autumn's leafy legacy. Bold daffodils nod golden heads, whilst closer scrutiny reveals the first shy celandines and wood anemones. Bird songs blend with the music of wind-strummed trees. Bright warmth alternates with soft showers.

I walk. Seeing and seen, hearing and heard, touching and touched. My feet feel the angles and textures of the land. My hands greet, caress and bless trees and shrubs. My eyes drink colours and patterns, light and shade, movement and stillness. My skin welcomes warmth and coolness in turn. My ears and eyes observe the courtship of birds, and the aerial dance as a crow repels a pair of buzzards. At times, I am stopped in my tracks by heart-aching beauty, or the call of a tree.

There is joy and gladness, a sense of oneness with all life, with Gaia. And there are darker feelings too. Grief for old trees, wise friends, felled by winter storms or a chainsaw. Anger at what we are doing to the Earth. Frustration at the slow pace of change, and how little I can do to speed it. Despair that *Homo sapiens*, this glorious experiment, seems bent on self-destruction. And reluctant acceptance that both yin and yang, positive and negative, are inseparable parts of life. Unless I open to the pain, I cannot experience the fullness of joy.

Our modern Western civilisation proudly and loudly proclaims that there is no meaning or purpose. Cosmos, Gaia and humanity just happened by pure chance through the outworkings of blind laws. And yet, beneath this sterile worldview, I sense a different reality. At the heart of all existence lies a deep Mystery. Why is there consciousness, matter and life rather than nothing? Where do they come from? I know in my heart, beyond all doubt, that a Spirit, a Consciousness, a creative Being dreamed the cosmos into existence for ineffable reasons of its own. I know I am an indissoluble part of this Whole. I know that, whether we wish to or not, we are still co-creating our world with each other and Spirit. And I know that our purpose and responsibility is to guide the evolution of humanity into the ways of love and wisdom, beauty and truth.

As I contemplate this inner, heart knowledge, I face the challenge of expressing it in ways that make sense to the rational mind. And I face the awareness that absolute truth—if indeed there is such a thing—lies far beyond normal consciousness. I grasp at strands blowing in the wind, glimpse flashes from facets of the infinite jewel, peer out at reality's wide landscape through a slit. And my perceptions are coloured by

THE FLOWERING OF SPIRITUALITY

my worldview, culture, beliefs, values, life experiences, and the structure and processes of my brain.

Wherever there is faith in THE truth, intolerance follows. Belief in the possibility of absolute truth is a gate through which evil enters the world. The Crusades, the Inquisition, Nazi and Marxist pogroms, genocide, the excesses of capitalism, the dogmatic claims of mechanistic science, terrorism ... Every form of knowledge, every religion, every perception brings gifts. But each is a single window onto reality. And there are many windows, many vistas, many landscapes.

With these provisos, let me try to explain my spiritual understanding. I experience Spirit in two ways that sometimes seem in conflict. One is Spirit as the transcendent source of all existence, the ground of all being, as ultimate reality. Spirituality, in this case, is about relationship with this source; about pursuing enlightenment, unity or salvation through meditation, prayer, ritual, devotion and service to the Divine. Many spiritual traditions proclaim this to be the highest path, the goal of which is to lose self in union with God, or in the ineffable experience of cosmic consciousness.

My second experience of Spirit is as my deepest inner nature—as 'the god within.' It flows from recognition that, if Spirit is the source of all existence, then I am embodied Spirit, and hence every aspect of my life and being is inevitably spiritual and cannot be otherwise. And similarly, every other being, every object, the whole of material reality is also a perfect expression and manifestation of Spirit. Spirituality in this case is about the sacredness of existence, and living an ordinary, everyday life in a sacred way. Possible spiritual paths and practices include creativity, vocation, conscious partnership and parenthood, aware consumerism, community life and service, connection with Nature and service to the Earth.

Sometimes pursuit of the transcendental path leads to a denial of life and the body, and an unbalanced asceticism. A similar lack of balance occurs when our material culture denies the spiritual nature of physical reality. For me, then, spirituality seeks balanced development of both the transcendent and immanent aspects. And it recognises that there are many possible spiritual paths from which we may choose.

Some of us may choose one path for a lifetime and emphasise either the transcendent or the immanent. Others of us may move from one path to another over time, or even follow several paths at once, with a more dynamic balance between immanent and transcendent. In my own case, my life encompasses elements of all of that, with a dynamically shifting emphasis over time.

This is how I see Spirit and spirituality now. But my perceptions are undoubtedly distorted and clouded, and may be different to yours. Perhaps I am mistaken. Perhaps in the future I will come to different conclusions. It is through openness to diversity, and the synthesis of all our perceptions that we draw closer to the truth.

\* \* \*

# FROM TRANSCENDENCE TO INSCENDENCE

### Niamh Brennan

*In imagination and dreams we transcend time and space,*
*in speech we transcend the limits of our body,*
*and in religion we transcend our humanity.*
—John M Hull

*It is not transcendence that is needed now but inscendence,*
*not the brain but the gene.*
—Thomas Berry

## Introduction

Transcendence is our capacity to go beyond the limitations inherent in matter. Life advances by moving beyond these perceived limitations and evolving new ways of being. This is primarily how a time-developmental Universe works. When we transcend we go beyond our experience into the realm of what is both there and not there yet. It is a bridge between the physical and the spiritual, the way in which they connect. It is the indication of possibilities and one of the ways we discover and learn about our capabilities.

But for the human at least, our desire and ability to transcend, innate or otherwise, has often blinded us to the sacredness that is inherent in the present. The idea of a transcendent God who is greater and other to this world, as well as Plato's Forms, have made us heedless to the divinity that permeates the Earth and forgetful of the fact that the Universe is the primary revelation of Divine mystery, even before scripture and even before prophets. Earth, as part of this Universal process and the part that is directly observable to us and that we participate in, is another form of divine revelation, a form that we can have immediate intimacy with and be present to, at our fingertips, under our feet, in the air that we breathe.

Passionist priest and cultural historian Thomas Berry made the distinction between transcendence and inscendence in one sentence. He wrote, as quoted above, that 'it is not transcendence that is needed now but inscendence, not the brain but the gene'. This sentence and its connotations struck me. If transcendence is what takes us beyond then inscendence must be what takes us 'in'. If transcendence takes us out of the physical world, then inscendence takes us back into the physical world.

Transcendence is experienced through consciousness, the mind or the psyche but our consciousness is shaped by the Earth. It is shaped through our senses of touch, taste, smell, sight and hearing. This is how the world comes to us. Our form and function as a species are also formed by the Earth, as is our imagination, as is our spirituality. Inscendence is deepening our relationship with the Earth that formed us, using our body and its senses to experience the divine through the natural world, being more present to it, noticing our connection and our dependency on it, noticing how it has shaped us and every other creature, every plant, every rock, noticing how it sustains us. To do this, we need to pay attention...

## Inscendence

The sun makes the world glisten, calls out the bees and butterflies, spreads joy. The colours of the flowers are brighter, more vibrant and defined, the white of the magnolia and the violet of the pansy, the yellow of the daffodil, they all seem much more visible under the golden rays of the sun, much more alive and present, much more here. And so it is with me. It draws me out, the sun, out into this sparkling, dancing world alive with creatures and the sound of bustling busyness tingling with excitement and noise and colour. It sings to me, the lightness of its spirit tickling all that it touches, so exuberant and free. In its rays I forget myself. Strange that the weather can do that to a person, make me forget myself, fill me with gratitude and light me up in much the same way that it lights up the sky, clearing me of the day-in, day-out niggles of existence. More than this, it makes me want to sing, to add my voice to the noise, a symphony of the sun on the utter joy of being. Even the wind seems more leisurely as it passes, less frenzied and pre-occupied. Under the sun it is a world of delight. Strange that the weather can do that.

The rain wets the world, each single, solitary drop finding its place, dispensing itself where it is called to be, in the narrow crevice of the rock, on the slender leaf the ant climbs on, into the open bosom of the tulip. Drop by drop it falls, moistening and softening the soil, releasing the scent of damp earthiness and making the world somehow more real and tangible. It lashes my face and wets my skin, bringing me back into my body, one physical element colliding with another, bodies of water breaking against bodies of flesh, reminding me of the physical nature of our existence, the vitality of life, its force and determination. It covers the sky in a rough grey blanket that is heavy and waiting to burst. There is excitement and anticipation in its coming, the promise of something, of freshness and cleanliness, the promise of water. It pours over the land and is consumed by it, its transparent mist clothing the woods, rivers and mountains in satin drapes of mystery, a reminder to me of the mystical splendour of life. And yet amidst this splendour, in the curious twist that is Nature's, its dark skies drag my thoughts into the eddy of myself, swirling and disconnected, heavy and brooding.

It amazes me still, the power of the weather to stir the human heart. And underneath this weather the throbbing pulse of life itself, of which the human heart is part, breathing through tree and blossom and bird and branch, the invisible thread of existence that we are all entwined in. The determination of the tiny hummingbird: the sleekness and stealth of the snake: the speed of the panther: the ingenuity of the spider: the grace of the dolphin: the patience of the turtle: the foolishness of the human…each creature so particular. Isn't it strange how nobody can be anybody else? A diverse and evolving world, a world of rain and sun, of flesh and thought. We can feel its mystery in the same way that we can feel the weather. It catches in our breast, this compelling beauty, makes us exhale and shake our head, robs us of our words while our hearts expand. We can watch its ways, the orange moon sinking as the earth turns its back on her, the sea rushing and collapsing upon the shore, the flight of the starling in flock. And this is our gift, all of this beauty and complexity that is weaving a magical story and our own eyes to see it and our own body to feel it and our own selves to participate in it.

And when we feel this gift of existence and the joy that is released with it, how do we give it to others? How do we learn to make it present, to pass it on in the same way the sun does, touching people tentatively, caressing us, making us smile, making us softer? It must be in us, no matter how deep it lies or how roughly it has been corroded by cynicism and bitterness, it must be in us because we are here and isn't joy at the root of what it means to be alive, and isn't life in its essence a celebration of existence, and just simply that? All we need do is think of a child to be reminded that there is something in the soul of our nature that bursts forth uncensored and uncritical, voices uplifted singing toward the stars, adding our voices because we are alive and we can, spilling our notes into the sky for the clouds to catch and release or do with as they may. Isn't that another gift of existence that it is played out day by day, second by second without our knowing anything of its plans in the deepest part of its nature?

It is often hard to believe that things are occurring, that they happen. The tricks of time that make a minute feel like a lifetime and a decade flash by leaving us reeling in its wake wondering where we were. The time that governs us is not the time of Life nor of this all-encompassing Universe. It unfurls at its own pace, some times rapid, other times imperceptible and yet with or without human measurement 'things change', places, people, ideas. The life force that runs through us, that we possess briefly, charges on towards its destination in its own resilient manner, running by its own internal clock that we have not yet learned to read or understand. Even as we invent our own ways of measuring and commit ourselves to always falling short, this life force unfurls at its own pace. It is greater than us and shows itself occasionally in a triumph of unexpected happening—an ocean from a rainfall, the development of a planet, a generously beautiful smile. There was a time that they were not and yet, here they are now, present and real, brief. To acknowledge this is to realise that every moment of life is different from the last and yet every moment is entwined with what came before it and what will succeed it whether we can perceive it or not; that every moment counts because we can contribute to how that moment will be. Isn't that in itself, amazing? Isn't that inscendence?

And so we walk whether it rains or shines, the feet of our bodies moulding the clay of the earth, crushing the grass. We let the wind rush through us, open our mouth and take it in. Breathe and blow it out again. We swim in the oceans pummelled deliciously by the waves. We smell the summer scents of lilac and roses, night-scented stock, the winter perfumes of pine and burning turf. The cold bites our hands, the sun burns our face but there is nowhere else we'd rather be than delighting in the Nature that sustains us, experiencing it. And we come to realise that there is something deeper occurring than just living on a planet, some sacred unfolding that is being born right before our eyes, right here, immediate and revealing itself to us, if we only have time to notice...

*I don't know exactly what a prayer is.*
*I do know how to pay attention.*
—Mary Oliver

\*    \*    \*

# PART SIX

# ELEMENTS
# OF GREEN
# SPIRITUALITY

*Earth*

# GOING TO GROUND

### Marian Van Eyk McCain

When I was five, my grandmother donated a little patch of her garden to me, and gave me sunflower seeds to plant. For ages, nothing happened. Then, tiny shoots appeared. I watched in amazement as the plants grew and grew until they were more than twice as tall as me, their huge yellow heads nodding over, way above my head. It seemed like a miracle. Well, it was, really.

Back then, I assumed that soil was just inert stuff that held the roots and supported the plant stems. No one told me otherwise. It was many years before I really understood what an amazing and important substance soil is, and how unappreciated and badly treated it is by some sections of humanity. Yet a good relationship with it can enrich our lives.

Dirt, soil, earth. The topsoil, the subsoil, the rock underneath. All our lives, we rest upon it. Depend upon it, literally, in all senses of the word. Yet if you think about it, we modern folk spend very little time with our feet actually touching the earth itself. Some of us might go a whole day or even a week without glimpsing bare soil. We can even forget that it exists. Much of the time, especially if we live in the city, between that soil and our feet lies the dead weight of concrete, sitting dully and heavily over earth that may never see the sun again. That always makes me feel sad. Although 1 know it is a silly fantasy, since builders always remove the topsoil before they build, I still have this image of some poor mole or earthworm struggling to the surface only to discover he or she has come up right under the middle of Safeway or the motorway or Gate 15 of the airport. It is a dilemma, for I need stores and roads and airports, too, just like everybody else does.

I also need the soil, for my life utterly depends upon it. Without soil, there would be no food, and without food we would all die. So it seems important to me to think about this dirt, this thing upon which all life depends.

Firstly, I believe we need to think about it in order to ensure that it is being properly taken care of and that there is enough of it that is *not* covered over. Lots of areas where the trees can grow and the moles and earthworms can still poke through the surface. And lots of it that are guaranteed never to be covered over—ever. Because land developers and builders—and governments—often don't notice when they are overdoing things and putting profit ahead of health and sanity.

Secondly, I think we need to look at our relationship with the soil from the point of view of having been created out of it, and being headed towards intimate reunion with it after our death. Realizing the importance of that relationship, we might want to put more emphasis on celebrating that deep connection. We might want to find opportunities in our lives to walk barefoot, to dig in the garden, plant things in the soil, smell it, get it on our hands. There is literally an earthy satisfaction for many of us in those things, a satisfaction which we may have forgotten in our busy lives up among the concrete buildings, and which will come flooding back when we walk barefoot along the beach or spend an afternoon on our knees in the garden, weeding and planting and mulching.

Thirdly, it seems important to consider the symbolic aspect of it. In other words, the necessity to stay grounded. Physically, we do this by remaining aware of our bodies and not ignoring or overriding their messages of weariness or pain. Emotionally, we do it by keeping a firm hold on reality and commonsense and by tempering drama with humour. And spiritually, we do it by honouring where we come from, our emergence from the 'stuff' of the Earth.

Soil is made up of three basic types of ingredients: minerals (the fragmentary particles of all kinds of rocks), humus and living organisms. The humus is composed of a vast conglomeration of once-living matter, the waste products of creatures, the broken down remnants of plant parts, all combined into a rich, nurturing compound, essential to continuing life. It is from this compound that seedlings draw their nourishment and build themselves into grass, flowers, trees—green and growing things which, in their turn, nourish and build the animals. Organisms living within this soil mixture—moulds, bacteria, worms and other creatures—make up the huge army of workers that convert the raw materials, like dead plant and animal matter, human and animal wastes, etc., into usable form. A huge army which, by the way, is still largely unstudied. It is an astounding fact that only a mere 5 percent of soil organisms have ever been described and classified even though, as Michael Colebrook points out in Part Seven, there are thousands of different kinds in every teaspoonful of soil. I always used to assume that scientists knew everything there was to know about soil, but apparently their knowledge is extremely limited.

Once all these decaying and putrefying materials are fully decomposed and turned into humus, they are sweet smelling, clean, beautiful and wholesome again. They eventually become the crumbly chocolate-colored compost into which we love to plant our daffodil bulbs.

But between the decaying, rotting matter and the sweet smelling compost there is a time gap—and, for most of us, an awareness gap. The process of transformation is slow and mysterious and takes place mostly in the dark. So we see the two ends of the process but not the middle. Only if we recycle everything ourselves can we get a sense of the whole cycle. But most of us throw our garbage in the bin and we buy the compost at the garden store and rarely if ever think about what lies between these two events.

Sadly, our familiarity with the earth, with the movement of things in and out of it, is something we have largely lost. Our loss of that familiarity and knowing, and the pollution of the soil by umpteen industrial and commercial processes that we know so little of, has separated us from that which is really the matrix of our existence. It has made us strangers to the earth and made of dirt a foreign and potentially lethal substance. In a way, we have become strangers to ourselves—to our own bodies and to their matrix.

The soil, and the rock below it, is the body of Planet Earth. The body with which we were born and in which we age is our borrowed piece of soil. We leave it behind us when we die, returning it to whence it came. So to me it makes sense that while it is in our care, we take good care of it. Like a library book, we should not trash it. Similarly, it behoves us to take good care of the Earth's body too, since everything else which lives depends on that. To me, there is a deep connection between the way we take care of our bodies and the way we take care of the soil and of the world. Start thinking about one, follow it far enough and it inevitably leads you to thoughts of the other two. Want to be more healthy? Improve your diet. Which means eat better quality, cleaner food—organic food. Which means healthier soil. Which means a healthier planet.

Our bodies *are* the soil, they *are* the Earth. As the Irish philosopher John O'Donohue so lyrically expressed it in his book *Anam Cara*, we are beings made of clay. "We so easily forget that our clay has a memory that preceded our minds, a life of its own before it took its present form. Regardless of how modern we seem, we still remain ancient, sisters and brothers of the one clay... The human body is at home on the earth."

So when my own grandchildren planted sunflowers, I had a lot more to tell them than my grandmother had told me. About the importance of soil, and the creatures who live in it. About the importance of nurturing and protecting it, for all our human sakes and for the sakes of all those non-human life forms with whom we share the planet. About its sacred nature. They needed to learn about humus. And about the huge, unthanked workforce of indefatigable beings who create the basis for new life out of the raw materials of death. A healthy patch of soil, I told them, is a huge, complex ecosystem in itself. An underground community. A vast co-operative project undertaken by billions and billions of tiny interdependent creatures, most of whom we neither see nor know the names of. All of them matter.

I hope the children listened.

*   *   *

*Air*

# TO MY SON WHO ASKS HOW I CAN PRAY TO THE POWERS OF AIR

Claudia Van Gerven

I t's not about air, it's about
breathing, how air
enters me the gentlest
of lovers, hovers above the small
of my back, penetrates
the most obscure air sacs.
And I am ungracious, simply expect
such pure streams
of faithfulness.
And the powers of earth, to invoke them
is to understand
at last how they hold up even this
city of glass, how dirt is still the level
above which vertebra
foolishly stack themselves.
We forget that we are simply given
water, each cell
a small sea. We are innumerable shorelines

from which foreign swimmers—
other creatures going
about their business—happily
thrive in the minutest corners
of what we are. And no,
I do not believe that the powers of fire
will come if I call them, they are here
already, they burn
in the sugar peas, the early lettuces.
They burn in me. I am
simply calling
my errant spirit home,
back to this bed of ice stars,
to this universe slowly
exploding, to my own cells
dying more rapidly than they unfold.
I am saying
I am here, where the winds pound
against the Flatirons, where sidewalks
buckle to the earth's
slow breath, where daffodils will flame
for an instant beneath the flood
of late spring snow.
I am not asking for anything
I have more than I can bear.

\*     \*     \*

*Fire*
# REKINDLING THE FLAME

## Victoria Field

---

W inter is a time to enter into the darkness, the place without light. There is still, we know, the fire inside us, the fire of life, perhaps reduced to a tiny glowing ember. We seek the fire outside ourselves, the radiance of a wood burner at the heart of a family home, the single bar of an electric fire, switched on only occasionally by someone lonely and housebound.

The darkness intensifies and Christmas and winter solstice celebrations use light and fire, red and glitter, feasting and festivities to remind us that the fire inside us still burns, that the sun will return, that a new born baby can change the world. But perhaps it's only later, when the snowdrops appear and we are aware that, yes, the days are lengthening, that we think, perhaps, winter won't last forever.

Easter is the central feast in the Christian liturgical year and doesn't have a fixed date in any civil calendar but is celebrated according to the progress of the sun and moon. Easter falls on the first Sunday after the Full Moon following the Spring Equinox, after which light outweighs darkness. Its timing and much of its symbolism is shared by the Jewish Passover and both have their roots in celebrations in honour of the Pagan Oestre, or Ostara, the Goddess of the Dawn.

At Truro Cathedral, the Easter Liturgy begins at 5.30 am, the darkest hour of the night. We come together, by car or on foot, along empty streets in a sleeping world, arriving in silence, not summoned by bells, and moving easily or slowly, we enter the dark forest of the cathedral. Familiar figures are shadowy, we can't see each other's faces and the cathedral's usually radiant windows are the blank black flatness described by the blind. Looking up, there's only darkness. The soaring pillars, vaults and arches, all the familiar structures are invisible. We are sleepy, only half-awake, vulnerable, hopeful, waiting for light.

Darkness is the comfort of the warm bedroom and the terror of the unloved child. Darkness is the silent wonder of woodland at night and it's the endless grey days of the bereaved or depressed. My tears have been my meat day and night. Sometimes, it's hard to trust that light will come. The winter's been long this year. Trees are still bare, waiting for the gentle green fuzz of leaf. The daffodils are stunted, primroses so far, few and far between and the wrens are silent. Walking away, or staying in bed, deep under the duvet, is always an option. Creation seems weary. Darkness is a time of memory, lying awake rerunning the days of our lives, the happiness and regrets, the asking in the small hours.

Why art thou cast down O my soul? The reading this morning takes us back to the words and concerns of the world before Christ. In this darkness, listening to a voice reading ancient words, we become one with those speakers and writers, and those that heard them. We are simultaneously in the present, in the past, heading to the future and eternity. All of us began in the darkness of our own private sea and we live with the mystery of what awaits. The Service of Light begins. Priests change their vestments, recalling the tradition of new clothes for Easter, one lost in our over-abundant Western world.

Fire is struck and the world is changed. As the watery light of dawn filters through stone and glass, our eyes are drawn to the flame. It is life, light, warmth, power. Like the sprinkling of small white stars on the bare twigs of the blackthorn, it changes everything. The light of Christ is passed from the Easter candle to those held by the congregation, illuminating faces and hands. Dawn is no longer hesitant, the monochrome becomes rainbows, the windows burst into colour and form. As the building fills with light, the Exsultet takes us back centuries and forward again into today, this Easter, the triumphant fanfare of the organ turning air into sound, light into music, moving straight into the singing of the Gloria, a harmony of human voices coming together, becoming one. The flame moving from hand to hand, passed on with smiles or eyes cast down is stripping death of its power. Everything contains its opposite. To be blessed is to be wounded. Only by dying back, can trees and flowers grow again.

The fire inside us is nourished and warms us and that warmth radiates to the world around us. But the Earth needs rain as well as sunshine. Now the ceremony moves from the heat of the eternal flame to the cool cleansing of water. Like parched flowers, we lift our faces to feel the gentle rain of baptismal water, sprinkled over the congregation like joy, like the sparkling spray kicked up by a child jumping the waves.

All over Cornwall, springs and holy wells are full, the hedgerows, fields and woodlands are ready to burst and bloom into spring. The winter's been long this year but already, lambs are suckling and there's the vanilla scent of gorse on the cliff paths.

At the end of the Eucharist, there's no doubt it is morning. Having come together in the dark, we leave the bright garden of the cathedral, its blazing candles, immaculate lilies, the rich gleam of its windows and soaring pillars, to head out into the world, rekindled, refreshed, moving from darkness to light, the fire inside us rekindled. Alleluia, alleluia.

*   *   *

*Water*
# GAZING INTO SPACE

Mary Kelson

Standing under the blackened, star filled skies in an Australian desert is an experience that imprints its essence into the very fabric of your embodied humanity. You simply can't forget it. It won't let you. The paradoxical moments of 'the grandeur of God' rhythmically dance and enmesh themselves with 'the God of the infinitesimal.' A body stands there in silent, songful awe, replete in singularity and complexity.

I live in South Australia, the driest state in the driest continent on Earth. I've been here for 26 years and am only now beginning to embody and understand this communion of place. I dwell in the land of the Peramangk people, in the beautiful hills wrapping themselves around the plains of Adelaide, plains that stand, sentinel-still, pointing towards the great northern deserts of Australia. Like many places on Earth our home, the element of water is foremost in our communal awareness. Its lack: its polluted and exploited states: its generosity: the drying of the springs: the greedy-eyed gaze on our aquifers: the salination of the great River Murray which once flowed into the oceans here; it no longer does, it simply does not have the will to do so anymore. It waits. Place grieves these losses with us, whilst it goes on generously evoking life.

In South Australia many people are becoming very aware of how water shapes the landscapes of life: something the First Nation peoples have always known and held, and still continue to do so. The Kuarna people of the Adelaide Plains have a story about an ancestral being, Tjilbruke ('hidden fire'), which teaches about the law and environment of the Kuarna country.

## Tjilbruke

On the shoreline at Kingston Park in Adelaide, stands a stone sculpture of Tjilbruke, a well known and respected man, tenderly holding the dead body of his favourite nephew Kulultuwi who was speared and murdered by his two half brothers Tetjawi and Jurawi out of jealousy. Kulultuwi had speared an emu (the emu his uncle was hunting) and broke the law. This gave his half brothers the opportunity to spear him.

When Tjilbruke heard of his nephew's death he found his body and carried it to a spring of freshwater on the beach at Ululkundank (Kingston Park). Here he dried and wrapped it and then headed south. Wherever Tjilbruke stopped to rest he thought about his nephew, burst into tears and a spring welled up on that spot. His weeping and grieving created seven springs along the coast. After Tjilbruke placed his nephew's remains on a ledge he went into the depths of a cave and emerged from it covered in yellow dust, then wandered some more around the land. He took a grey currawong, rubbed its fat on to himself and tied its feathers to his arms. He flew into the air and became what is known as a glossy ibis. His spirit continues in these birds and is closely attached to swamps and springs. His body became a rocky outcrop of iron pyrites at

Barunkungga, becoming a constant source of hidden fire, the meaning in his name.

With a small group of people, I recently stood at the foot of this sculpture and listened to the Tjilbruke story. I sat alone by the very same spring and I drank that water. It was my simple gesture of acknowledging and participating in the story and tradition of this place known in Kuarna as Ululkundank. I know I can't belong here in the same way as the Kuarna people. I can't stand there in that space and even attempt to know it, understand it or belong to it as if it were my own space; this type of belonging is not right. However I can stand in that space and feel and listen and express my own experiences of being there.

It is amazing, really, that this spring still flows. It is quite beautiful. The grieving and the tender regard for Tjilbruke's nephew is still held and expressed in a landscape that is now urbanised and changed. The spring simply flows, and evokes a re-'membering', a constant presence asking me to listen deeply and respond to life from patience and compassion, not reaction and rescue. This may sound very simple but sipping from that spring was—and is—a pivotal moment in the journey and place of my own life. Water is a bearer, an *evocatuer*, a storyteller and story-shaper of landscape and life.

### The Spring I live Beside

I live by a spring. I've been here for only five years. I remember the day this place captured me. As I stood at the bottom of the pathway gazing into the greenery, something was beckoning me. My friend pushed me up that bricked pathway, knocked on the door and the conversation began. This place claimed me; it wanted me here. I know that in my bones. I don't understand it, I simply intuit it. I often sit alongside the spring and wonder.

There seems to be very little recorded or accessible information regarding the first people who are the custodians of this land, the Peramangk people who walked this country for some 50,000 years. I have learned to sit and listen and renounce my compulsion to rationalise and know. Many people visit my home and while they are sitting in the garden, sometimes aware of the spring, sometimes not, I watch their faces soften and become gentler, their bodies relax. Such is the presence and beauty of the hidden flowing water within this place. This spring shares in our lives and shapes our experiences. It somehow holds us in our grief and despairing moments; it is a well, weeping and laughing with us. Through bad droughts and the emergence of bores around it, the spring is still flowing, sometimes just and sometimes with a fecundity. Maybe my job is to witness its story and to tell it; that's our friendship.

This wellspring keeps me present to the wellspring behind my own hope and despair for the future of this Earth and my fear of the destruction of her living systems.

### A Simple Reflection

How do we tell the stories when some of them seem too painful to tell and to listen to? How do we hold this 'place' in the same way it holds us? Who do we choose to be in this world? What is possible and who cares for the possible?

Australia's star filled, blackened skies, the wisdom and stories of this land's First Peoples captured in the Tjilbruke story, and the springs that burst into this dry landscape and give life enable me, and remind me to turn my gaze into an interior place, a place behind the drivers of hope and despair. To a place of being in the here and now. Not a denying place but a fully present place, vulnerable, real and a little willing to hold and feel all the tears of the world, just like the springs do. Jesus of Nazareth called it 'living in the reign of God.'

The springs I sit with, the stories that come by me and the stories I tell, the people and living creatures I know; the beauty, the terror and the art evoked in the communion of living place, open my heart a little at a time and soften the hard within. I am grateful for this.

\* \* \*

# EMBRACING THE ELEMENTS

## Marian Van Eyk McCain

A s I write this, the trees stand leafless against a pale, winter sky and cold fingers of wind, straight from Siberia, pry and poke at the cracks and gaps in my cottage walls. It is a time to huddle indoors. Indoors, we are warm and dry. Indoors—or so we tell ourselves—we are protected from the elements.

But wait, which 'elements' am I 'protecting' myself from. Earth? Air? Fire? Water? Right now, the woodstove burns to keep me warm. I am breathing air in order to keep alive this body which is composed of 80% water. The food I eat comes from the earth in my garden. I *am* the elements. My life utterly depends on them.

Outside my window, a robin perches on a twig, feathers fluffed against the chill. I look out on green fields, criss-crossed by hedgerows. I walk every morning along country lanes, through woods, along a path beside a stream. How lucky I am, people tell me, to be able to spend so much time out in Nature.

'Out in Nature'—now there is another thoughtless cliché. Another of these lazy, crazy habits of language that shape our worldview and that we, in turn, pass on to our children. For Nature is not 'out there'. It is in here also. Its rhythms pulse and throb through our arteries, its liquids bathe our cells, its moods and energies surge, sizzle and sigh within us. Just like the oysters that open and close their shells with the tides, our bodies and spirits respond to the cycles of morning and afternoon, day, night and season.

For too long we have listened to the mechanistic language that draws us farther and farther away from who and what we really are: cells in the body of a living Earth, as dependent on that Earth for our existence as our faces and fingers are dependent on our beating hearts. We have been like sleepwalkers, moving with closed eyes towards a precipice. But at last, and maybe only just in time, we are beginning to wake up.

When James Lovelock did the simulation experiments to prove that our planet, with its ability to self-regulate, behaves exactly like one huge living organism, he stopped short of actually stating that it *is* a living organism. As a scientist, he knew that such a claim is unprovable within the current limitations of our science. Yet for millions of people, including me, Gaia Theory, as it is now called, was the biggest 'aha!' of the twentieth century. Not only did it chime with the native wisdom of many of the world's indigenous peoples, it called to something we knew and felt deep in our bones: a sense of ultimate belonging, a feeling of love and identification that goes way beyond the enjoyment of a beautiful scene or an unexpected meeting with a wild creature of another species.

Furthermore, it made perfect, elegant sense. It was Arthur Koestler who first coined the term 'holarchy'—a system in which each part is a 'holon.' i.e. both a part of something bigger and a whole composed of smaller parts. The cells of my body are made of smaller parts (intracellular organisms) which are composed of even smaller parts (molecules) and so on, all the way down and in. My cells are holons of my body's organs, the organs are holons of a greater whole that I call 'me'. I am a holon in one of the ecosystems which make up the body of planet Earth, which in her turn, is a holon of the solar system, which is part of the Milky Way galaxy and so on, all the way up and out.

So what if we lived our lives with this understanding at the centre? What if humans, especially in the industrial North, were to let go of the anthropocentric (human-centred) way of thinking which has brought us down this path towards the precipice of ecocide and began to think ecocentrically instead? What if we fully acknowledged our total dependence on Gaia and her elements and came to the realization that Nature is not only around us but also within us and that we are cells in the body of a living planet?

The anthology *GreenSpirit: Path to a New Consciousness*, which I edited, demonstrates how switching from an anthropocentric to ecocentric attitude will affect every one of our society's institutions—medicine, law, economics, education and so on. Above all, it shows how to restore meaning to our lives. For a GreenSpirit way of seeing the world is not based purely on the pragmatic need to develop a sustainable way of life for humans in order to prevent ecological collapse. It also grew out of the hunger for meaning, for a deep sense of connectedness and for a spiritual dimension to *everything* we do and feel and experience—the way we live, eat, work, play, celebrate and carry out all the functions of our day. Only when that deeper meaning is restored to our lives can we ever feel completely whole and happy. And only then can we do our part to change things for the better, working from the heart rather than the head, doing our part from passion and love of the Earth to which we all inescapably belong.

\*    \*    \*

# PART SEVEN

# HOW, THEN,
# SHALL I LIVE?

# THE NATURE OF PRACTICE

## Marian Van Eyk McCain

F rederic and Mary Ann Brussat, authors of the book, *Spiritual Rx: Prescriptions for a Meaningful Life*, describe practice in the following way:

> *Practice has always been the heart and soul of the world's religions, and it is also the distinguishing characteristic of today's less organized spirituality movements. It can be something as simple as lighting a candle or a ritual as complex as a Native American vision quest. It can involve the spontaneity of a Christian's flash prayers in the street or the rigorous structure of a Muslim's five-times-a-day prayer. It is Africans and Sufis expressing their yearning for God through dance, Jews studying the Torah, Buddhists doing mindfulness meditation, and Hindus looking for divine signs in common objects.*
>
> *The variety of practices matches the diversity of human personalities. Many connect with the Holy through the mind while others emphasize the body or the emotions. Some prefer group worship; others, private prayer. A person's daily practice might include elements of ethical training, emotional transformation, motivational change, physical exercise, community building, study of sacred texts, and acts of service. Practices attend to every mood and moment.*
>
> *Many of us, however, were raised to think of spiritual*

*practice as little more than a short grace before meals, saying
bedtime prayers, and going to a weekly worship service. The
problem with seeing practice this way is that it can become
just another entry on our already crowded To Do lists, one of
those frequently unexamined routines of our daily life. Practice
degenerates into an onerous obligation similar to taking out the
garbage or flossing our teeth.*

*A far more useful and rewarding approach is to view
practice not as an activity we do but as the path we travel
on our spiritual journey... everything we do is practice. As
the Zen Buddhists put it, how you do anything is how you do
everything. Walking down the hall mindfully is as important
as sitting on the mat in meditation. How a Christian acts at
work on Monday is as significant as attendance at church on
Sunday. You don't step on the path of practice for a few minutes
a day, then jump off to go about the rest of your life.*

So how do we practise green spirituality? My answer is
that we practise it first through our attitude towards the Earth
and second through the manner in which we live our lives. The
second, of course, flows logically from the first. When we see
ourselves a part of a living Earth we move from an attitude of
egocentricity to one of ecocentricity. In a living ecosystem, the
integrity of the ecosystem has priority over the selfish needs of
any individual and at the same time all individuals are precious
parts of the whole. So in every decision he or she makes, the
greenspirited person automatically asks "might this harm the
Earth?"

In order to know the answer, we need to educate ourselves

about the Earth and its needs. Which means we have a duty to become what the late Michael Colebrook, our next contributor, calls 'Earth-literate.'

\*     \*     \*

# WHAT DOES IT TAKE TO BE
# EARTH LITERATE?

## Michael Colebrook

*I swear there is no greatness or power that*
*does not emulate those of the earth,*
*There can be no theory of any account unless it*
*corroborate the theory of the earth,*
*No politics, song, religion, behaviour, or what not, is of account,*
*unless it compare with the amplitude of the earth,*
*Unless it face the exactness, vitality,*
*impartiality, rectitude of the earth.*
*All merges toward the presentation of*
*the unspoken meanings of the earth.*
—Walt Whitman. *A Song of the Rolling Earth.*

On Aldous Huxley's *Island*, Mynah birds fly about saying "Attention," reminding the humans to walk though the world in full awareness of what is going on around them. This is a form of awareness that is able to appreciate—and where possible understand—the hidden meanings of the Earth.

Ursula King has coined the term 'Earth Literacy' to describe the area of understanding needed to achieve this level of awareness.

A major problem with Earth Literacy is that there are

many aspects that stretch our faculties to breaking point. It is probably true that most of what happens on and in the Earth is either too small or too big or too fast or too slow to be within the scope of our unaided senses.

For example: in one square meter of productive soil one could find 10,000,000,000,000 bacteria, 10,000,000,000 protozoa, 5,000,000 nematodes, 100,000 mites, 50,000 springtails, 10,000 rotifers and tardigrades, 5,000 insects, myriapods, spiders and diplurans, 100 slugs and snails and maybe one vertebrate such as a mole. From that mole to the five thousand insects and spiders, these are visible to the naked eye. For the next four categories—the rotifers to the nematodes—you would need a low power microscope: for the remainder, which contains by far the most abundant groups, you would need at least a good high power microscope and special preparation of the material in order for them to be visible at all. And this just tells us what is there. What they all do and how it all fits together to make soil is another matter.

An example at the other end of the size scale is the weather. What we experience as weather is a strictly local manifestation of a global and extremely complex system involving the whole of the atmosphere as well as the oceans and the land masses. As John Muir came to realize, "When we try to pick out anything by itself, we find it hitched to everything else in the universe."

What is involved is a level of knowledge that is positively daunting and which takes time and effort to acquire and cultivate. It is also a life-long process.

I will begin with what I call epiphanies. By this I mean particular events that have a permanent and profound effect at a personal, individual level. The problem with epiphanies is that you cannot plan them: they just happen. It is possible to expose oneself to situations of potentiality, but that is about all that can be done.

Possibly the most valuable form of epiphany is to find yourself in a situation where you feel that the world is totally indifferent to your existence. Henry David Thoreau encountering the boulder field which forms the summit of mount Katahdin in America wrote,

> *And yet we have not seen pure Nature, unless we have seen her thus vast and drear and inhuman... Nature was here something savage and awful, though beautiful. I looked with awe at the ground I trod on... It was Matter, vast, terrific, not his Mother Earth that we have heard of, not for him to tread on.... There was here felt the presence of a force not bound to be kind to man.*

The value of the scary epiphany is that it helps us to recognise our true place in the scheme of things and teaches us not to have an over-inflated sense of our significance.

There are also epiphanies with a high 'wow' factor. Annie Dillard writes about one of these in her book *Pilgrim at Tinker Creek*.

> *About five years ago I saw a mockingbird make a straight vertical descent from the roof gutter of a four-story building. The mockingbird took a single step into the air and dropped. His wings were still folded against his sides... Just a breath before he would have been dashed to the ground, he unfurled his*

*wings with exact, deliberate care, revealing the broad bars of white, spread his elegant, white-banded tail, and so floated onto the grass. The fact of his free fall was like the old philosophical conundrum about the tree that falls in the forest. The answer must be, I think, that beauty and grace are performed whether or not we will or sense them. The least we can do is try to be there.*

I can begin to share Annie Dillard's experience: a couple of years ago I saw a magpie do much the same thing. It was from the top of a tall tree and the bird had to fly out a short distance before it could fold its wings and go into free fall. The whole event took just a few seconds. I just happened to be looking in the right direction at the right time. "The least we can do is try to be there."

There are other forms of knowledge that contribute to Earth Literacy and possibly the most important is to get to know something about your locality.

I suggest that our sense of place is greatly enhanced if we know something about the rest of the reality we inhabit and especially about how we share it with the non-human world.

When I was a biology student quite a lot of our practical work was involved in exercises in 'what is it and why?' We were presented with a specimen which could be anything in any of the kingdoms of living organisms and we were given the task of identifying it to the lowest level in the taxonomic hierarchy that we could manage. It is obviously asking far too much for this to be a universal accomplishment but on a limited scale, and relating to our immediate surroundings, it is a significant component of what we should aim for. At the very least we can know our birds and our butterflies, also our trees and the more common flowers. We can follow the biological seasons, be aware of what comes when and where.

We should also have a feel for the local topography. I live in Plymouth which is a city in the south-west of England bounded East and West by river valleys, on the North by the granite mass of Dartmoor and on the South by the sea. This undoubtedly has a significant impact on the city as a whole and also on the people who live here.

Coupled with topography is the geology of the area. As Plymouth is in the county of Devon it is not surprising that most of the rocks in the area of the city were originally formed in the Devonian period (417 to 354 million years ago). It was a warm period, with average sea levels of 180 metres above the normal. What is now the land of Devon was then at the bottom of the sea and situated much closer to the equator than it is now. But there is an extra piece to the story. The bedrock of my garden is shillet, which is like a low grade slate. It is a metamorphic rock: one that has been transformed by extreme heat. The heat came from a massive intrusion of molten rock which happened at the end of the Carboniferous period about 300 million years ago. The rock subsequently cooled and formed the granite mass of Dartmoor.

One of the classic routes to knowledge about the natural world was to acquire collections of things. Charles Darwin was an avid collector and he regularly took his children on collecting expeditions. I don't doubt that the collecting habit has introduced many budding naturalists to the wonders of Nature. As a botany student I was expected to acquire a herbarium of pressed and dried specimens of the more common local plants. But not everybody can do this. At the entrance to a nature reserve I remember seeing a notice which said "Leave nothing but footprints. Take nothing but photographs." It has to be something like this.

We are blessed in this country in having the BBC Natural History Unit with its steady production of excellent films and TV programmes covering many aspect of the natural world. We can take advantage of the endless patience of the camera people which enable us to see, albeit at second hand, so much that we would be very unlikely to see otherwise. There is the problem that the approach of the film maker is inevitably selective, picking on the aspects of the natural world that can be captured on camera and which the producers hope will arouse the interest of viewers. The little creatures, of which there are many, tend to be left out.

Reading books, watching television or surfing the internet can only ever provide the infrastructure to Earth Literacy and a preparation for the essential activity of experiencing the natural world at first hand. A lot can be achieved by staying in the comfort zone of the sign-posted path, the guided walk and the organised excursion. And there is no shortage of organisations, societies, field clubs and groups of all kinds providing such opportunities. They play a major role of nurturing Earth Literacy. But there is a need for more.

John Lester-Kaye tells of an occasion when he was caught out in heavy rain:

*I took shelter under a birch tree but knew it was useless, I gave up and walked on; better to get wet properly than to be sodden in bits. At least I had the satisfaction of experiencing what everything else was having to endure. I have often thought mankind scuttles for cover too quickly—another separation from the wild world. We habitually shun discomfort as though it was always bound to be bad for us, whereas if we stuck it out it might bring us closer to Nature and provide some insight to the deeper truths of our place on Earth.*

He is saying we need sometimes to let the wild be wild and we shouldn't run away from it or pretend we can control it.

I suggest we might be able to claim to be Earth Literate when we have achieved a proper estimate of our place in the world and of our location in reality.

*   *   *

# WHERE IS YOUR PLACE?

## Marian Van Eyk McCain

Our 'place in the world' can of course be anywhere. It may be in the country or if may be in the heart of a big city. Emma Restall Orr, a prominent member of the Pagan community in the UK reminds us that Nature is everywhere, not just in the countryside. And Nature is not always pretty. She writes:

*In any religious tradition where nature is revered, nature is understood as both beautiful and brutal. Nature's fabric is (self) crafted upon the weave of its own laws and logic, and some of those are far from beneficial to humanity: nature is neither just nor is it merciful. Secondly, though, and importantly here, nature includes human nature, and the most fleeting glance at human nature reveals how harsh and difficult that can be...*

*This is as relevant in the city as anywhere else. Forces of human nature are more prominent inside the city than outside of it, and these can be more intrusive, provoking our empathies through reflection and distraction. Yet it is no less crucial that we learn how to work with the gods of human nature: anger, hunger, lust and fear which are as affecting as the gods of the winds, sun, rain, or fertility.*

*We can honour nonhuman nature, nurturing it within the concrete jungles of our planet, but each day we must also learn how to better inspire our fellow humans, making sure that what we add to the currents of human nature is positive. Instead of dismissing and avoiding our species, here there is essential work for us to do. Where there is desolation, we can sing stillness; where there is rage, we can dance those present into creativity; and so on.*

*So find the currents in the city, the forces and flows, the eddies and tides ... of crowds and traffic, in human noises, human creativity, human interaction, emotions, colours and energies. Nothing is negative or inherently evil, there is potential inspiration, positivity, in everything. Our task is to find the current, feeling how we are a part of it, how we might influence it, bringing joy and wakefulness to its flow.*

And Stephan Harding, in his book *Animate Earth* suggests that we find one small corner of our world to serve as our special place.

*One of the best things you can do to promote your own mental health is to find a special place outside where you can go on a regular basis to connect with the animate Earth. If you live in a city, this may be your own back garden or yard, but if you live in the countryside you will almost certainly have access to a variety of inspiring places in your immediate surroundings. Wherever you are, your task is to search for a place where you can spend time exploring and deepening your relationship to the great living being that is our planet.*

*Make sure that you allow yourself to be guided by your sensing, feeling and intuition when you are looking for your special place—let your thinking take the back seat. You'll know that you've found the right place if it provokes a profound sense of pleasure in you (perhaps even a feeling of overwhelming beauty), if your senses tingle with amaze¬ment at its sheer loveliness. Pay attention to how the place works on your feelings. Choose a place that evokes an easy comfort in you, and notice how the place speaks to your intuition—is there a numinous 'aura' that connects you to the psyche of the place, to a sense of its animate presence? Lastly, let your thinking mind consider the logistical viability of the place—is it too far for regular visits, will it offer you enough privacy and quiet, what clothing and footwear and other outdoor gear will you need to make your visits peaceful and comfortable?*

*Develop a rapport with your place by visiting it regularly— allow it to communicate its subtle messages of colour, scent, taste, touch and sound. As you let yourself be known by your place, learn to converse with it, gleaning its subtle meanings much as you would enjoy a conversation with a close friend.*

\*  \*  \*

# CREATIVE SPIRIT

Joan Angus

I am in the air we breathe.
I am in the sun which lights our day,
shining through leaves of trees.
I am in the moon which moves the tides,
 and the stars traversing the night sky.

I am in the earth, feeding the seed
which grows, flowers, wilts and dies
to become earth.
I am the pollen on the bees' knees,
fertilising the flowers to make those seeds
growing into plants which feed us
and trees which provide the air we breathe.

I am in the birdsong, the tigers' stripes,
the fishes' gills, the dewdrops on the spider's web;
I am the diversity of life forms, the life cycles
of living things, the balance of nature.
I am the flowing of the river, the colours
of the rainbow, the soul of the rock.

I am the laughter in your eyes.
I am in your joys, sorrows, hopes and fears.
I am in your health and sickness.
I am in your anger and you are in mine.
You are in my peace and I am in yours.
When you love me, then you love yourself.

We are in the music we make, the words we say.
We are in our dreams and schemes;
the houses we build, the children we birth.
When we abuse any of these treasures we abuse ourselves.

When we kill, we kill ourselves.
We are the Universe, changing and renewing,
constantly flowing, enfolding, enriching, sustaining.

*   *   *

# ABOUT THE
# CONTRIBUTORS
# AND FURTHER
# RESOURCES

# ABOUT THE CONTRIBUTORS

**Joan Angus** is a retired occupational therapist with a passion for wildlife, gardening, writing, sewing and circle dancing,

**Niamh Brennan** is a freelance writer on spirituality and cosmology and has published in several theological journals including 'Spirituality' and 'The Furrow' as well as the IMU quarterly. She has also contributed to the Liturgical Website of Emmaus Productions. She currently works as the Education Officer with the Green Sod Land Trust giving workshops to children on the Story of the Universe.

**Brendan Caulfield-James** is a former teacher and holistic therapist. On leaving school, he joined a religious order, subsequently working in Hong Kong, Malaysia/Singapore and Australia. He studied the Mystics with Thomas Berry, Matthew Fox and Brian Swimme and has a Masters in Spirituality.

**Michael Colebrook**, who died in April 2012, was for many years the Production Editor of the GreenSpirit Journal. A scientist all his life, his working career was devoted to research on the planktonic ecosystem of the North Atlantic Ocean and the North Sea.

**Janice Dolley** lives in Gloucestershire and is Development Director for the Wrekin Trust who are building an alliance of organisations towards 'One Spirit'; a trustee of the Findhorn Foundation and member of the core group of CANA (Christians Awakening to a New Awareness). The conference gathering "Into Christ Consciousness" came out through a collaboration of these organisations together with Friends of Iona and Contemplative Fire.

**Victoria Field** is a writer and poetry therapist based in Canterbury, Kent, UK. She runs groups and teaches nationally and internationally. She writes poetry, short fiction and drama and has co-edited three books on therapeutic writing.

**Claudia van Gerven** is a published poet.

**Malcolm Hollick** lives in 'retirement' in Hobart, Australia, where he is associated with the Pachamama Alliance, transition Tasmania, and efforts to establish new ecovillages. From 1998-2010 he lived in the Findhorn Community, Scotland during which time he wrote *The Science of Oneness: A worldview for the twenty-first century*. More recently, he co-authored with his partner, Christine Connelly, *Hope for Humanity: How understanding and healing trauma could solve the planetary crisis*.

**Mary Kelson** lives in Adelaide, South Australia She is an educational consultant working with adults and young people in broadening their awareness, understanding and literacy in sustainability and community. Mary is a storyteller and writer with a particular interest in the untold stories of religious women and stories that grab the heart.

**Emily Kimball** is a speaker, author and longtime outdoor enthusiast who takes lessons learned from her adventures and applies them to everyday life.

**Alison Leonard** has been exploring green and goddess spirituality for over ten years, is a Quaker and writes fiction and poetry.

**Marian Van Eyk McCain** is a retired psychologist and the author of seven books. She edited the anthology *GreenSpirit: Path to a New Consciousness* (Earth Books, 2010) and is also co-editor of the GreenSpirit Magazine, a free-lance writer, columnist and blogger.

**Susan Meeker-Lowry** is a writer, organic gardener, and herbalist who lives in Maine, USA. In addition to numerous articles, she is the author of *Economics as if the Earth Really Mattered* and *Invested in the Common Good* (both from New Society Publishers). For nine years she published the journal *Gaian Voices: Earth Spirit, Earth Action, Earth Stories*. (Full color PDFs and a limited supply of B & W printed versions are still available from Susan). Susan currently offers a line of herbal skin care products through her home-based business, Gaia's Garden Herbals. Many of the products are made with herbs, flowers, barks, and buds grown in her garden or wild-harvested nearby. They are all natural and mostly organic, made in small batches with love.

# FURTHER RESOURCES

For details of all the contributors to this book and links to their website, plus information about other titles in this series and where to get them, please go to:
**www.greenspirit.org.uk**

\*   \*   \*

# GreenSpirit
## *magazine*

GreenSpirit magazine is free for members and is published in both print and electronic form. Each issue includes essential topics connected with Earth-based spirituality.
**Find out more at www.greenspirit.org.uk**

*"For many of us, it's the spirit running through that limitless span of green organisations and ideas that anchors all the work we do. And 'GreenSpirit' is an invaluable source of insight, information and inspiration."*
– JONATHON PORRITT.

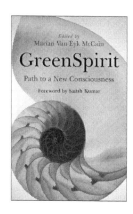

# GreenSpirit

*Path to a New Consciousness*

**Edited by Marian Van Eyk McCain**

Only by bringing our thinking back into balance with feeling, intuition and awareness and by grounding ourselves in a sense of the sacred in all things can we achieve a new level of consciousness.

Green spirituality is the key to a new, twenty-first century consciousness. And here is the most comprehensive book ever written on green spirituality.

Published by Earth Books
ISBN 978-1-84694-290-7
282 pages

# Meditations with Thomas Berry

*With additional material by
Brian Swimme*

**Selected by June Raymond**

Selected and arranged by June Raymond, especially for GreenSpirit Books, this is a collection of profound and inspiring quotations from one of the most important voices of our times, the late Thomas Berry, author, geologian, cultural historian and lover of the Earth.

Published by GreenSpirit
ISBN 978-0-9552157-4-2
111 pages

# GREENSPIRIT BOOK SERIES

I hope you have enjoyed reading this little book as much as I have enjoyed editing it. And since it is the introductory volume in an ongoing series, I hope that it has whetted your appetite to read more in this series and discover the many and varied ways in which green spirituality can be expressed in every single aspect of our lives and culture. Thus, for example, we have a whole book devoted to looking more closely at the art and skill of 'living green' and all the ways that we can, every one of us, make a difference in the world by downshifting to a sustainable lifestyle. Even more importantly, it provides ample evidence that far from being a hardship this may be one of the most enjoyable and spiritually satisfying things you have ever done.

Some other examples of 'applied green spirituality' can be found in the GreenSpirit book series.

For more details visit **www.greenspirit.org.uk**.

*    *    *

# Other titles in the GreenSpirit book series

*All Our Relations: GreenSpirit Connections with the More-than-Human World*
Edited by Marian Van Eyk McCain

*The Universe Story in Science and Myth*
Greg Morter and Niamh Brennan

*Rivers of Green Wisdom: Exploring Christian and Yogic Earth Centred Spirituality*
Santoshan (Stephen Wollaston)

*Pathways of Green Wisdom: Discovering Earth Centred Teachings in Spiritual and Religious Traditions*
Edited by Santoshan (Stephen Wollaston)

*Deep Green Living*
Edited by Marian Van Eyk McCain

*The Rising Water Project: Real Stories of Flooding, Real Stories of Downshifting*
Compiled by Ian Mowll

*Dark Nights of the Green Soul: From Darkness to New Horizons*
Edited by Ian Mowll and Santoshan (Stephen Wollaston)

*Awakening to Earth-Centred Consciousness: Selection from GreenSpirit Magazine*
Edited by Ian Mowll and Santoshan (Stephen Wollaston)

**More details on GreenSpirit's website**

Free for members ebook editions

O our Father, the Sky, hear us
and make us strong.
O our Mother, the Earth, hear us
and give us support.
O Spirit of the East,
send us your Wisdom.
O Spirit of the South,
may we tread your path.
O Spirit of the West,
may we always be ready for the long journey.
O Spirit of the North, purify us
with your cleansing winds.
~ Sioux prayer

\*   \*   \*

Printed in Poland
by Amazon Fulfillment
Poland Sp. z o.o., Wrocław